MICROSOFT DYNAMICS NAVISION Frequently Asked Questions: MS Navision FAQ

Compiled by Terry Sanchez-Clark

MICROSOFT DYNAMICS NAVISION Frequently Asked Questions: MS Navision FAQ

ISBN 978-1-60332-005-4

Edited by: Farrah Stewart

Printed in the United States of America

Please visit our website at www.itcookbook.com

TABLE OF CONTENTS

I. INTRODUCTION: NAVISION 7

II. CONFIGURATIONS & CUSTOMIZATIONS 10

Question 1: Client/server architecture...................... 11
Question 2: Running Navision from command prompt
.... 11
Question 3: Importing SIC codes...............................12
Question 4: Navision slow in opening any process ...13
Question 5: Dataport crashing Navision 3.7.............14
Question 6: Menu suites 15
Question 7: Importing company logo into Dynamics
NAV 4.0..15
Question 8: Hijri date conversion.............................16
Question 9: Importing accent characters 18
Question 10: Filtering item list OnLookup..............19
Question 11: Connecting Navision 4.01 to SQL 64 bit
....21
Question 12: Navision Attain 3.01b and Vista.......... 22
Question 13: Navision C/AL 23
Question 14: Exporting to Excel 24
Question 15: NAV 5.0 vs. Vista vs. SQL 2005........... 25
Question 16: New user password............................. 26
Question 17: Zup file directory................................. 27
Question 18: Login error – Session DB 28
Question 19: NAV customization.............................. 29
Question 20: Printing C/AL code 30
Question 21: Error uploading license to SQL server
with NAV4SP3 31
Question 22: Inserting problem (SQL2005 –
NAV4SP2)... 33
Question 23: CFRONT and STX 34
Question 24: Using SP2 objects with SP3 executables
.... 35
Question 25: Importing .fib 36
Question 26: Customer comments 37

Question 27: Navision 2.6 and C/ODBC 38
Question 28: Q78: Navision toolbar error when opening Outlook 39
Question 29: RAID 1 or RAID 10 for native NAV database 40
Question 30: Scroll bar problem - NAV4.0 SP1.........41

III. COMPATIBILITY, TECHNICAL REFERENCES & CLARIFICATORY QUESTIONS 42

Question 31: Searching for technical overview to Outlook integration in NAV 5.0................................ 43
Question 32: Expense Allocation............................ 44
Question 33: Objects version.................................. 45
Question 34: Citrix and NAV 4.0 45
Question 35: Corrupt ZUP files 46
Question 36: Microsoft 2007 & NAV 4.0SP3 compatibility... 47
Question 37: Changing the Windows color 48
Question 38: Export Data to Excel 49
Question 39: NAV 5.0 kitting doc............................ 50
Question 40: Monitoring Navision C/Site DB Space 52
Question 41: Restoring the Backup 53
Question 42: Navision 3.7 and Vista........................ 54
Question 43: NAV 4.0 SP3 and Windows RTM Vista55
Question 44: Client-Server problem in Vista 56
Question 45: Navision unstalling 57
Question 46: Adding or removing granules from a license temporarily 58
Question 47: Potential customer 59
Question 48: Assigning Navision after going out of business..61
Question 49: Using two printers............................. 62
Question 50: Opening a Folder from a database field 63
Question 51: Adding a new path to current system path 64
Question 52: Disaster recovery................................ 65

Question 53: COM automation and Navision outstreams (BLOB export).......... 66
Question 54: Setup checklist.......... 66

IV. NAVISION APPLICATIONS 67
Question 55: Reports currency format 68
Question 56: Purchase order archive.......... 68
Question 57: MIS postings in analysis by dimension 69
Question 58: Filtering.......... 69
Question 59: Removing invoices from suggested payment list 70
Question 60: Opening invoice in MS Word.......... 70
Question 61: NAV 3.7 copy &'paste' does not work... 71
Question 62: Availability of system generated field for all tables 73
Question 63: Calculating multiple VAT 73
Question 64: Building sales portal.......... 74
Question 65: Aging inventory 74
Question 66: Formatting 75
Question 67: Transaction number 75
Question 68: WIP reports.......... 76
Question 69: Year end closing 77
Question 70: Identifying & purging inactive customers 79
Question 71: Downloading journal entries 80
Question 72: Closing sales orders 81
Question 73: Error 1355 82
Question 74: Posting invoices problem 83
Question 75: Invoice issue: "Sell to Cus #" 84
Question 76: Applying cash 85
Question 77: Inventory 86
Question 78: Inventory value <> 0 when item quantity = 0.......... 87
Question 79: Changing Properties during runtime .. 88
.... 88
Question 80: Mixing text & expression in a text box 89
Question 81: Line amount before discount 90
Question 82: G/L post & print NAV 3.70 client 91

Question 83: Modifying sales invoice header 92
Question 84: Editable Field on a Non-Editable Form
.... 94

V. NAVISION REPORTS & TABLE FORMATS 95

Question 85: Check Stub on top 96
Question 86: Displaying Contents of a Table-Field .. 96
Question 87: OptionCaption on an option type field
from a table 97
Question 88: Drawing a line on a report 98
Question 89: Footer question 98
Question 90: Editable property 99
Question 91: Limitations on part storage 100
Question 92: Exporting table reference information
using dataport 101
Question 93: Data Import 102
Question 94: Importing MS Access 102
Question 95: Copying and pasting from Navision to
Excel 103
Question 96: Security and domain groups 106
Question 97: Creating order records automatically. 107

VI. NAVISION SOFTWARE INSTALLATION, UPGRADES,
AND TOOLS 108

Question 98: Installation of Navision 2.6 109
Question 99: Migration tool kits 112

INDEX 115

I. Introduction: Navision

Navision has gone through several name changes since 1995. Currently, it is marketed by Microsoft as Microsoft Dynamics NAV. Its previous names include "Navision Financials", "Navision Attain", and Microsoft Solutions Navision Edition". All these refer essentially to the same product.

Microsoft Dynamics NAV is an enterprise resource planning software intended to assist small and medium-sized enterprises with finance, manufacturing, customer relationship management, supply chains, analytics and electronic commerce. Its cost-effective solution can easily be tailored for any company. It can support customization and add-in software to meet industry or other specific needs. Moreover, it can adapt as a growing business needs more power and functionality.

Microsoft Dynamics NAV addresses the following business needs:

Financial Management	Record and store financial records in a central general ledger that includes charts of accounts, balances, VAT reporting, and more. It allows you to define your preferred currency, create accounting periods based on your fiscal and business cycle, manage bank accounts and cash, and automate routines such as check-writing and bank statement reconciliation.
Manufacturing	Manufacturers can respond quickly to customer demands and improve manufacturing performance by automating and improving processes such as production-order management, supply and capacity planning, visibility into shop floor operations, and graphics-based production schedules.
Business Intelligence	Turn raw data into understanding of how a business is operating. It allows you to choose from basic to advanced analytics functionality, provide decision makers with a 360-degree view of performance, and set up graphical reports and displays using an interface similar to Microsoft Outlook 2003.

Sales and Marketing	Put customer information at the fingertips of managers and employees to help your people build better customer relations. It manages contact information, organize sales campaigns, identify sales opportunities, automate sales tasks, and set up automatic reminders.
Distribution	Microsoft Dynamics NAV gives businesses a flexible solution for solving distribution challenges. It can be used to track and manage inventory, including in multiple locations; get up-to-date information about in-stock quantities; implement better warehouse management, including tailored pick orders and stock replenishment by pre-set thresholds; and get real-time data regarding inventory and shipments.
Integration with your systems	Microsoft Dynamics NAV is designed to work smoothly with other Microsoft products such as Microsoft Office Suite, Microsoft SQL Server 2003, and Microsoft Windows 2000 and XP. Its commerce portal capabilities also allow a company to create a Web site to work easier with customers and partners. It can also be integrated with a wide range of other software products, so that even if a small business has already substantial IT infrastructure, it can be used with Microsoft Dynamics NAV so that a business makes the most of its IT investment.

II. Configurations & Customizations FAQs

Question 1: Client/server architecture

We are developing a customization to Navision and my research into Navision's client/server options has produced mixed results. I know with Axapta that one can have a server that has all of the application objects, and the clients can just connect to the server and grab any of these objects to execute as needed.

Is there something similar to this in Navision? Or will our customers need to import our objects on every client machine?

A: No, you do not need to export the objects to your clients' machine. All you have to do is to install one server and all your clients would have to connect to that server.

Question 2: Running Navision from command prompt

I want to run Navision upon signing in into a remote server with the remote desktop connection.

What is the executable command line I can use for this?

A: You can find the command line parameters by looking at the 'Installation Section' of the Configuration Manual. In there are the various parameters. It is in the DOC folder of NAV product CDs.

Question 3: Importing SIC codes

I have a comma delimited list (and excel file) of SIC codes and I want to import them to become Industry Groups.

Is there something that I can do get them in one batch rather than entering each one manually?

A: You will need to access Object Designer and then design a simple 'Dataport' to import your codes into the Industry Group table. Have a look at an existing Dataport (maybe 5901 - Import IRIS to Fault Codes) to see how they hang together.

Question 4: Navision slow in opening any process

I find Navision to be slow in opening any process even for just one user. And I have about 30 users on the system. It takes two to three minutes to move from screen to screen. I have deleted before the *zup* file and it worked fine for two days. Now, when I delete the *zup* file, it does not make it better. What else can do? Could anyone help me?

A: There are many things that you can look at, such as the following to mention a few:

1) How are your users connecting to the system, i.e., 10/100/1000 or citrix or rdc?
2) The SQL or native database and its size
3) The server specs, i.e., the RAM, number and type of disks and the type of raid your using.
4) Customizations with bad code
5) The version you are using and whether you have all the updates
6) SQL tweaking if that is what you use.

If you are using a Native database, you can check the Object Cache / DBMS Cache for the database on the server.

Question 5: Dataport crashing Navision 3.7

We utilize the dataport in Navision to import data on occasion. Recently, we are experiencing problems with some of the dataports. Sometimes they work fine. At other times they crash Navision on the client and a dialogue box asks if I would like to send an error report. The DP starts and runs in part before crashing. It ran several times on the same unchanged file but crashed at a different percent each time. It does not seem to be the file because after a crash, it still works on the following attempt. By the way, it happens in many machines and even happens on our VAR on some occasion.

How do I fix this?

A: If you are experiencing it in just one particular machine, first delete the *zup* and then give it a try. Second, go to Tools → Options and then increase the cache. Third, if all else fails, reinstall the client. But before reinstalling the client, delete the *zup* and increase the cache first and observe if it happens again.

Question 6: Menu suites

I am taking over a project that customized Navision. The menu suite that we use for our customization is at the Partner (80) level. But since this number is not in the range where we have our unique IDs, I assume that it is possible that a customer would already have a menu suite at the Partner level. Is this accurate? And if so, I would think they would have to merge our code for the menu suite with their existing code. Is this also accurate? Could anyone elucidate on this?

A: Yes, it is accurate. If the installation has customization by another partner, it would have 80 level menu suites. Also, when you need to provide an update, it is better to use that 80 level existing menu suite and then add your items to that.

Question 7: Importing company logo into Dynamics NAV 4.0

Does anyone know what dimensions the .bmp file should be for importing a company logo into Navision?

A: In "Company Information" table - field Picture is a type Blob, it says: "A BLOB (Binary Large Object) is a complex data type. Variables of this data type differ from normal numeric and string variables in that BLOBs have a variable length. The maximum size of a BLOB is normally determined by your system's disk storage capacity. However, the maximum size in C/SIDE is 2GB."

So there is no strict size in terms of dimension. You could set it in very large dimensions as long as it is still visible. So play around with the size until it fits your needs. But if you want it to look good, try to set the dimension at around 200 x 100 or smaller.

Question 8: Hijri date conversion

Could anyone explain to me the process of converting Gregorian to Hijri dates?

Could I use it in Navision?

A: The answer is yes to both questions. If you can put together the logic behind the conversion process then it should not be too difficult to write a function to convert a date from Gregorian to Hijri and store this as a text field in your required database table.

In NAV, you can hyperlink to these pages with a button.

If you want to create your own or a new code unit, you could use the function below.

Call the Date2Hijri function with a Date and the format you want returned.

Format=0 will return the date in this format: 29/10/1421
Format=1 will return the date in this format: Thursday 29 Shawwal 1421 A.H.

You should be able to get it working using the code below.

New function: Date2Hijri(Date : Date;Format : 'integer') : Text[80]

```
    d := DATE2DMY(Date, 1);
    m := DATE2DMY(Date, 2);
    y := DATE2DMY(Date, 3);

    IF (y > 1582) OR (y = 1582) AND (m > 10) OR (y = 1582)
AND (m = 10) AND (d > 14) THEN
      newDate :=
        GetIntPart((1461 * (y + 4800 + GetIntPart((m-14) / 12 ))) /
4) +
        GetIntPart((367 * (m-2-12 * (GetIntPart((m-14) / 12 )))) /
12) -
```

```
        GetIntPart((3 * (GetIntPart( (y + 4900 + GetIntPart((m-
14) / 12)) / 100 ))) / 4) + d - 32075
    ELSE
      newDate := 367 * y - GetIntPart((7 * (y + 5001 +
GetIntPart((m-9) /
7))) / 4) +
        GetIntPart((275 * m) / 9) + d + 1729777;

WeekDay: = GetWeekday (newDate MOD 7);

l := newDate - 1948440 + 10632;
n := GetIntPart((l - 1) / 10631);
l := l - 10631 * n + 354;

j := (GetIntPart((10985 - l) / 5316)) * (GetIntPart((50 * l) /
17719)) +
      (GetIntPart (l / 5670)) * (GetIntPart ((43 * l) / 15238));
l := l - (GetIntPart((30 - j) / 15)) * (GetIntPart((17719 * j)
/50)) -
      (GetIntPart (j / 16)) * (GetIntPart ((15238 * j) / 43)) + 29;

m := GetIntPart((24 * l) / 709);
d := l - GetIntPart((709 * m) / 24);
y := 30 * n + j - 30;

CASE Format OF
    0: EXIT (STRSUBSTNO ('%1/%2/%3', d, m, y));
    1: EXIT (STRSUBSTNO ('%1 %2 %3 %4
A.H.', WeekDay, d, GetLunarMonth (m), y));
    END;

New function: GetWeekday (Day: Integer): Text [30]
    CASE Day OF
      0: EXIT ('Monday');
      1: EXIT ('Tuesday');
      2: EXIT ('Wednesday');
      3: EXIT ('Thursday');
      4: EXIT ('Friday');
      5: EXIT ('Saturday');
      6: EXIT ('Sunday');
    END;

New function: GetLunarMonth (Month: Integer): Text [30]
```

```
CASE Month OF
  1: EXIT ('Muharram');
  2: EXIT ('Safar');
  3: EXIT ('Rabi I');
  4: EXIT ('Rabi II');
  5: EXIT ('Jumada I');
  6: EXIT ('Jumada II');
  7: EXIT ('Rajab');
  8: EXIT ('Sha"ban');
  9: EXIT ('Ramadan');
  10: EXIT ('Shawwal');
  11 : EXIT ('Dhu"l-Qa"dah');
  12: EXIT ('Dhu"l-Hijja');
END;
```

Question 9: Importing accent characters

We are having a problem importing CSV text files using a dataport into Navision 3.6 that is using a Native database. The Navision language is US English (When you go to TOOLS->LANGUAGE).
The CSV files contain some accented French characters and I have changed the code page in Windows to be French. Now, when I run the characters either do not show or are translated into incorrect characters. Could anyone provide suggestions on what to do with regards this issue?

A: Try saving the file to ASCII first before importing it in Navision using a text-editor (for example: www.textpad.com). If you find this rather difficult, try this code unit which you can use to convert a string from ANSII to ASCII and vice versa: http://www.mibuso.com/dlinfo.asp?FileID=287.

Question 10: Filtering item list OnLookup

I have added two fields in Transfer Order, namely Production Order No. and Item No. After selecting the Production Order Number, the item number is filled (production order "source number."). The Transfer Lines display only those items which are at the component list of the item in the header and not all the items. Does it mean that the item list is filtered for the item in the header? What is the explanation for this?

A: You could try something like this OnLookup on the Item No. field on the Transfer Line table.

```
TransferHeader.GET ("Document No.");
IF TransferHeader." Item No." <> " THEN BEGIN
  Item.GET (TransferHeader." Item No.");
  IF Item." Production BOM No." <> " THEN BEGIN
    ProductionBOMLine.SETRANGE ("Production BOM No.",
Item." Production BOM
No.");
    ProductionBOMLine.SETRANGE (Type,
ProductionBOMLine.Type:: Item);
    IF ProductionBOMLine.FIND('-') THEN REPEAT
      ItemFilter: = ItemFilter + ProductionBOMLine." No." + '|';
    UNTIL ProductionBOMLine.NEXT = 0;
    IF ItemFilter <> " THEN BEGIN
      ItemFilter: = COPYSTR (ItemFilter, 1, STRLEN (ItemFilter)-
1);
      Item.SETFILTER ("No.", ItemFilter);
    END;
  END;
END;

ItemList.LOOKUPMODE (TRUE);
ItemList.SETTABLEVIEW (Item);
IF ItemList.RUNMODAL = ACTION::LookupOK THEN BEGIN
  ItemList.GETRECORD (Item);
  VALIDATE ("Item No.", Item." No.");
END;
```

The above should work and should point you in the right direction. A couple of points though to consider:

ItemFilter could possibly flow over the maximum size for a filter. You might want to put something in place to handle this. Also, if you have multi-level BOMs, you would need to write some recursive code to handle that.

Question 11: Connecting Navision 4.01 to SQL 64 bit

Is the configuration Navision 4.01 on 32 bit Windows XP connected to SQL 64 bit on Windows 2003 54 bit supported by Microsoft? I would like to use the Windows Integrated logins.

Is this possible? Will it work?

A: It is possible to connect Navision to SQL servers in 64 bit. Remember that there are 2 different versions: IA64 (Itanium) and X64 (Xeon or AMD). SQL 2005 supports both and SQL 2000 only supports IA64. Navision can connect to any of these 32/64 bits. Just use xp_ndo_ia64.dll or xp_ndo_x64.dll on your SQL server instead of hte xp_ndo.dll. You can find these files on partner source or with the entity that sold you Navision.

If you are using Windows Authentication when connecting to SQL server, you will need to use the xp_ndo.dll in order to connect using Windows authentication. Now with the 64bit OS, NAV has two DLLs that are used; IA64 (Itanium) and X64 (Xeon or AMD). This setup should work and is supported if you have the correct xp_ndo.dll (64bit) deployed using Windows Authentication.

Question 12: Navision Attain 3.01b and Vista

Does anyone know if Navision Attain version 3.01b is supported on Windows Vista?

A: Microsoft only supports Navision 4.0 SP3 (with platform update) on Vista. If you want to use a previous Navision version, you will have to do a technical upgrade (upgrade Navision server and clients to 4.0 SP3 (+ platform update) and keep using the existing 3.01B database). It does not look different if you only do a technical upgrade. The menus will still be the 3.01 menus.

Question 13: Navision C/AL

I am new to C/AL coding and I am trying to put some conditional formatting in a report. The following code does not work:

IF WOLINE.Price = 0 THEN CurrReport.SHOWOUTPUT:=True
Else
CurrReport.SHOWOUTPUT:= False;

Neither does this:

IF WOLINE.Type ='Charge' THEN
CurrReport.SHOWOUTPUT:=False;

I have never used WOLINE.GET or WOLINE.FIND.

Where should they be used in the context of what I am trying to accomplish?

A: We presume there is somewhere a WOLINE.GET or WOLINE.FIND in your code. Try this:

CurrReport.SHOWOUTPUT (WOLINE.Price = 0);

And this:

CurrReport.SHOWOUTPUT (NOT (WOLINE.Type ='Charge'));

If you define a record-variable WOLINE, you need to retrieve the record value somewhere in your code, usually with a rec.GET or rec.FIND statement. If you do not retrieve the record value, your record-variable will be empty. Try the OnAfterGetRecord-trigger for the data item you are using in your report.

Question 14: Exporting to Excel

How could I export the Detail Trial Balance report?

I can select "print to excel" on the Options of some of the other reports, but not this one and I need it.

How can this be done?

A: If this option is not available, then it needs to be developed. Alternatively, you could use the "Save as HTML" option when printing reports (using File → Save as HTML after starting the report) and try to open this in Excel.

You can also use a third party product, for example: www.print2excel.com.

Question 15: NAV 5.0 vs. Vista vs. SQL 2005

I have installed NAV 5.0 on Vista with SQL 2005. Initially, everything went fine. But, when I try to select a database in NAV, I get the following error message:

"The trace flag 4616 is not set on the server "machine name". You must set this flag and restart the server before you can connect using Microsoft Dynamics NAV."

Can you provide me ideas on what I am supposed to do with that?

A: As part of your SQL Server installation you should probably do the following:

01.) Open the Start Menu;
02.) Go to Microsoft SQL Server 2005 Group;
03.) Go to Configuration Tools Group;
04.) Click on SQL Server Configuration Manager;
05.) Click on SQL Server 2005 Services;
06.) Right-click on SQL Server ($INSTANCENAME) and click on Properties;
07.) Click on the advanced tab;
08.) Go to Startup Parameters;
09.) Enter the string so that it looks as follows (notice the end is the only change;
10.) Program Files\Microsoft SQL Server\MSSQL.1\MSSQL\DATA\master.mdf;-eC:\Program Files\Microsoft SQL Server\MSSQL.1\MSSQL\LOG\ERRORLOG;-lC:\Program Files\Microsoft SQL Server\MSSQL.1\MSSQL\DATA\mastlog.ldf;-T 4616;
11.) Click OK;
12.) Restart the SQL Server service;

Question 16: New user password

If we were on NAV 4.0 SP2 with SQL 2005, I can create a user in NAV and it automatically creates the user in SQL Server, not knowing what password was used. This password should be known; otherwise we would go all the time to the SQL Server to assign a new password to the new user.

How can I fix this?

A: If you are talking about Database logins, you should create the login under SQL Server Management Studio, then create the matching login under NAV and then assign correct user roles etc. In fact, trying to create a database login (under NAV) where a matching SQL login for that database does not already exist should produce a sync. error.

If you are using Windows logins, then you can create the user in NAV which will create a matching SQL user. There are no passwords to worry about in this scenario. Also, make sure you are using the correct authentication method when trying to connect to NAV from your users' client machine. For example, if you are actually using Windows logins but trying to connect to the database using Database Server Authentication, then the user would be asked to provide a password. This could be what is causing the confusion.

Question 17: Zup file directory

I need to change the directory of the zup file. I want it saved in a shared folder for each user on a server.

Can you guide me on how to change the file's directory?

A: You can do this by changing the shortcut on each user's desktop. Open the Properties page for the NAV shortcut and change the target to include the location of the zup for that user, e.g,

"C:\Program Files\Microsoft Business Solutions-Navision\Client\fin.exe" id=c:\zups\user1\user1.zup

In your case, you would have to replace the local path on C: to a network location. Just repeat this for each user. The next time they open NAV, it will create a zup file in the location specified.

Question 18: Login error – Session DB

I gave our Company Treasurer, the following roles configuration:

- ADCS: ALL ADCS User
- ALL: All users
- G/L-ACCOUNT: Read G/L accounts and entries
- G/L-BANK ACC: Read bank accounts and entries
- G/L-JOURNAL, POST: Post G/L journals
- G/L-PERIODIC G/LL: periodic activities
- G/L-REGISTER: Read G/L registers
- INTRASTAT-PERIODIC: Intrastat periodic activities
- P&P-VENDOR: Read vendors and entries
- S&R-CUSTOMER: Read customers and entries

However, he gets the following error:

"The Session Table does not exist as the required object name of NAVDB.dbo.Session in this database."

I have read on one site (only one) that this might be a bug, supposedly fixed under service pack 2.

When I do not add hte ADCS ALL and ALL roles to the Window's Login, he gets an error about table 2000000004 not existing. If I give him the 'Super role' the error goes away.

Is this a problem with me not assigning all the necessary roles? If so, then what else do I need to add? Or, is it a bug? Could somebody elucidate on this?

A: You are receiving the error "The Session Table does not exist as the required object name of NAVDB.dbo.Session in this database" and when you give the user ADCS ALL and ALL roles to the Windows account you then errors about table 2000000004 not existing.

There is a fix for this that was rolled up into NAV 4.0 SP1 update 3 and NAV 4.0 SP2 update 1. You can find your version by going to Help → About Microsoft Business Solutions-Navision and double-click on the text "Version 4.0 ..." and a dialog box will pop up giving you the build function.

Question 19: NAV customization

I am a software developer trying to evaluate NAV. Do we customize NAV in C/SIDE or can we do it in

, which is our preference? Is there a way to customize from Visual Studio 2005 like GP has? Is there a URL somewhere that lists business layer functions that are available within NAV that could be called from .NET?

Can you expound on this to clear up the issue?

A: All customizations are done in C/AL Code, using the C/SIDE development environment. There are ways to access the data from outside Navision, but the business logic is executed "inside" the Navision environment.

Starting from version 5.1, you will see a compiled .NET DLL being generated. But this cannot and should not be modified. Let us hope that version 6.0 brings some Visual Studio development options.

Question 20: Printing C/AL code

I was able to print the C/AL for an object only once. I have tried numerous times since then without success. Clicking the print icon in the upper left side of the window does nothing.

What am I doing wrong? How can I fix this?

A: If you have a developer's license (or a license with developer granules), you would be able to export the objects in text-format. Otherwise, you will have to copy the code to your favorite text-editor for printing. If you do not have an access to the source, you can use the debugger to have the source code displayed.

Question 21: Error uploading license to SQL server with NAV4SP3

I have received a license file for a client and now at the rollout stage would like to save the .flf file into the database to prevent users from manually setting it, or even having a shortcut to it, etc. So we select this 'Save License to Database checkbox' and a dialog box comes up where we pick the license file but an error comes up saying the following:

"You do not have permissions to perform 'License for DB'. Ask your administrator about permission settings. Translation may not be exact from the Russian version of NAV.

The user under which we attempt to do it with happens to be the SQL Server System Administrator and was also the same user in the Administrators group of the server. So permission-wise, it should be okay. Moreover, in NAV itself, this user is declared as a SUPER role.

The license file itself indicates having the SQL Server Option granule, which we specifically asked for when we placed the order. Has anyone else come across such a problem? Does it look like a license file issue or am I missing something when trying to upload it?

A: The ability to save the license to the DB requires granule 2020 that you must purchase. But It is required only if you intend to run more than one Navision database on the same server; not just test v live but two independent databases with different granule stacks.

For running an individual database in the same SQL Server, first deselect the option of saving the license in the database in File → database → alter. Then go to Tools → License → and select upload. This will load the license to the server.

To simply "upload" the license to the server, go to License Information, then select import the client license file, and then press Upload. This process places a copy of the license on the server which would become active for all users. There is no need for the users to know where it is saved or have access to the license file.

Question 22: Inserting problem (SQL2005 – Navision 4SP2)

We have a problem with a duplicate key using the instruction code "IF [table].INSERT THEN;". We get the error after running the following codes:

```
FOR i: = 1 TO 3 DO BEGIN
  ItemUoM.INIT;
  ItemUoM." Item No.":= Item." No.";
  ItemUoM.Code:= Item." Base Unit of Measure";
  ItemUoM." Qty. per Unit of Measure":= 1;
  IF ItemUoM.INSERT THEN;
END;
```

The insert instruction does not ignore the insert when the record is already in the table.

How can we fix this?

A: You would have to change the code to If Not Get Then, i.e,

```
If not ItemUoM.get (Item." No.", Item." Base Unit of Measure")
then begin
  ItemUoM.INIT;
  ItemUoM." Item No.":= Item." No.";
  ItemUoM.Code:= Item." Base Unit of Measure";
  ItemUoM." Qty. per Unit of Measure":= 1;
  ItemUoM.INSERT;
END;
```

If you are writing a dataport, add the code above the validation of base unit of the measure on the item.

Question 23: CFRONT and STX

I am wondering where the cfront looks for the fin.stx file. I installed cfront and tried to run the sample.exe but I got the following error message:

"The country code in the license file does not correspond to the country code (XX) in the STX file.
Exception Handler called with Fatal Error: 3. "

I have a license file with country code of XX. I have already copied the fin.stx from the ENC folder to the Navision Client folder, but the error persists. The same thing happened to my self -developed cfront application. I am running NAV 4.0 and everything is installed by default.

How can this be resolved?

A: The cfront normally determines the path to the Navision client from the registry. You can override this by using the DBL_SetNavisionPath () function.

There are many differences in NAV 4.0 CFront releases depending on the SP installed. In SP1, Cfront looks for the NAV client directory in the Win registry while it looks for the directory in the setnavisionpath () in sp2 and in the "current" directory. Moreover, this could further change by Cfront build to any variant.

To solve your problem, try any of the following:

1. Change the regional settings
2. Remove the NAV language directory
3. Replace the stx in the language directory to W1 stx
4. Expand the license
5. Rename the ENU folder to something else.

Question 24: Using SP2 objects with SP3 executables

I am working on a customization to Navision. The client says he is using NAV 4.0 SP2 objects with SP3 executables. What exactly does this mean and how does this affect how I develop the solution? Can you enlighten me on this?

A: This should not affect your development customization. However, you might want to use a 4SP2 database and 4SP3 fin.exe/finsql.exe in your development environment to ensure that your changes will work in the clients database.

You should always develop using the same executables as your customer. You get a copy of their database, or at least their objects, but you must use the same executables as your customers. Most of the time, it will not cause big problems if you don't but when the problems begin, they are pretty big.

Question 25: Importing .fib

I am new to Navision and I am having problem importing / inserting .fib files.

How can this issue be fixed?

A: If you do not know how in the first place, you should not do any importing. Nevertheless, you can go to Tools → Object Designer → File → Import.

Question 26: Customer comments

The comments on the Master record are quite useful for tracking notes and conversations regarding the record. For instance, the Customer Comments are typically used to record "collection activities".

It would be most useful if the notes were displayed with the most recent comment (based on date) first, and the oldest comment displayed last. The form should continue to support the entry of new comments, with a current date. Those comments should then appear first in the list.

The comments across the system (customer comments/contact comments, etc...) should likewise support text wrapping between the lines. This would be very useful for entering information that will take up multiple lines of text. Also, this should support pasting text into that comment sheets that would otherwise not fit.

Is this possible? Could anyone enlighten me on this?

A: Because of the way comments are implemented, this is not possible. It requires a complex logic to make it work. The solution would be to have a text BLOB to store the comments, and the existing table just to contain the index.

Question 27: Navision 2.6 and C/ODBC

Does Navision 2.6 come with the C/ODBC driver, permitting external applications to access the Navision database? Is there any difficulty I should anticipate when using Sun's JDBC-ODBC, Bridge Driver?

A: The answer is yes on both questions. On the NF 2.6 CD there is a folder with the ODBC-driver. But to be able to use this ODBC-driver your license file must first contain the ODBC-granule. You should really consider upgrading to a newer version for many reasons. One reason is that there is a bug in the 2.6 ODBC-driver with big amounts. It goes wrong if you have more than nine digits and some values get transferred the wrong way.

Question 28: Q78: Navision toolbar error when opening Outlook

I have NAV4.0 SP3 installed on my computer and have just installed NAV 5.0 on my computer. During the installation, it gave me an option of not uninstalling the old Navision and install NAV 5.0. I followed that option.

Now, every time I open Outlook, a Navision Toolbar Error message always comes out that reads as follows:

"The File int.etx was not found. Copy int.etx from the Navision installation CD to the client subfolder of the Navision program folder."

What should I do now?

A: All you have to do is to copy that file from your old Navision 4.0 SP3 client directory to the new client directory.

Question 29: RAID 1 or RAID 10 for native NAV database

I have a long time client who is running Navision 4.0 NATIVE (not SQL) with a 26 GB database in two separate parts using RAID 1. Each part is on its own physical set. They are upgrading their server and were going to use the same scheme, but the hardware vendor insists that using two RAID 10 sets would be faster than two RAID 1 sets. All of the official Microsoft documentation I can find only suggests RAID 1 for native Navision databases.

What is your advise on this issue?

A: Since it is a Native install, the best way to go is to use RAID 1. However, you should read the document "Hardware Guide for Microsoft Dynamics™ NAV 4.0 (Version 3) for details on RAID 10. In part, it mentioned that "RAID10 will be introduced as an alternative to RAID 0+1 (Storage section).

For two Raid 10 sets, you will need at least 8 hard disks (2*4). It will be faster than using 4 hard disks (two Raid 1 arrays). A 22 GB native database using three Raid 1 arrays works fine. The raid system is configured as a duplex raid, so it that it would not crash if one SCSI channel will be reset.

Another way is to split the database into 4 parts and then going with 4 RAID 1 arrays. This would give you the same number of disk as the RAID 10 solution but twice as many disk processes.

Native Navision does its own striping across disks, hence the recommended use of RAID 1 rather than RAID 10. In the real world, you would simply have to test it, but you can use 8 x RAID 1 arrays on one of your databases and 6 x RAID 1 arrays on the other. When you think about it, it doesn't make sense for Navision to stripe the data across disks and then the RAID controller to stripe the data too! So suspect that the hardware supplier is not familiar with Navision and it's striping, hence their recommendation for RAID 10 and not simply RAID 1. Now if it is SQL, it would be a different story.

Question 30: Scroll bar problem - NAV4.0 SP1

Does the scroll bar problem wherein the length scroll bar is not adapted to the actual number of records in an overview screen supposed to be solved in 4.0 SP2 or will be solved in 4.0 SP3?

A: You would experience this problem if you are using SQL. When opening an overview form from a native Navision database, all records are loaded and the scroll bar is reliable to the number of records. In SQL however, this is different because only a part of the records are loaded, i.e. only a CountApprox is done and not a Count. This explains the wrong proportion of the scroll bar vis-à-vis the number of records.

III. Compatibility, Technical References & Clarificatory Questions

Question 31: Searching for technical overview to Outlook integration in NAV 5.0

a) Where do I get the add-in file?

b) How do I install the add-in file?

A: In the client installation CD you should have a folder named Outlook. Install it and you should have the add-in in outlook.

Question 32: Expense Allocation

In short, I want to allocate the electric bill across multiple departments. I can set the departments up as dimensions, and set up a recurring journal to define the allocation percentages. What I am trying to do is have everything set up so I can just print a check and have everything post through properly to both the balance sheet accounts and the expense accounts?

Will this be a multi-step process, or is there a way to make it all happen in a single procedure?

A:. In standard Navision, this is a 2 setup process.

1. Post your expenses from the vendor
2. Print the check and pay the bill

If it doesn't go through A/P, then it would simply be a payment to your expense G/L account.

It's entirely possible to automate the posting of the expense account through A/P when printing checks through modification in Navision. However, you should consult with your VAR and have a clearly defined design specification written so no unexpected surprise comes up.

Question 33: Objects version

Is the version in "Help → About" the version for the objects or the executables? And if that is the version of the executables, how do I determine what version of objects a person is using with their Navision? Could anyone enlighten me on this?

A: Version 3.10B (3.60) means that the database is 3.10b and the executables are 3.60. You can check the version of each object in Tools → Object Designer.

Question 34: Citrix and NAV 4.0

We physically separated our distribution center from our HQ building. We are using Citrix for our communications with our users and their workstations. It seems that everyday there are printer issues. Our Net Admin has to go to the center and restart all of the machines.

Is there a better way to do this?

A: Service Pack 2 and 3 have many fixes and you should add them to your system. There is a setting in Citrix that tells it to remember the last printer you used in a session.

Question 35: Corrupt ZUP files

Our company is currently running Navision 3. I am not the Navision Admin but the server/domain Admin. A majority of our users connect to our Navision system through our Citrix servers. The Application Administrators constantly asks the Server Administrators to go in and delete the Citrix users ZUP files. They get reports of printing issues that they blame on a corrupt ZUP file. And deleting the ZUP file always solves the issue.

However, I feel that we are treating a symptom and not the cause. What seems to cause this constant corruption of these ZUP files? How should I deal with this issue?

A: In Version 3.7B, a fix was made regarding zup & Citrix. So if you are using a Navision version that is older than that, upgrading your executables might be the best solution. If that is not the case, then here are some posts about creating a separate zup file for each citrix user so that they would not have to reset and if the problem keeps on happening to just one person's zup, then you can narrow down the problem.

If it always seems to be a problem with the printer, you may want to think about re-installing the printer and its driver and make sure that the driver is the most updated one available.

Question 36: Microsoft 2007 and NAV 4.0SP3 compatibility

When trying to send an email message from NAV I get the following error:

"This message is for C/AL programmers:
Could not create an instance of the OLE control or Automation server identified by
GUID={03BC4F50-2ABB-48B3-B2A6-3F08EB1D013E}
1.7:{F3B45F48-1F4A-40C9-8DE6-5CC377BF4F82}:'NS Outlook Synchronization Handler'.OSendMail.
Check that the OLE control or Automation server is correctly installed and registered."

The standard object codeunit 347 complies without a problem and the above function works fine with Outlook 2003. Could anyone explain this problem?

A: Your problem seems to be an error of INTERFACE. Try re-installing the Navision toolbar for Outlook from the Client setup.

Question 37: Changing the Windows color

We have two databases on our system. One is our Live DB and the other is a Test DB. I normally have both DBs open at the same time. Often, it is very easy to make a mistake which DB I am working in and am looking for a way to change the visual appearance of the windows in the Test DB. Instead of the basic windows blue, I want to use red.

How I can have two different color schemes for each DB?

A: It depends on which version of Navision you are using. With versions < 4.0, you can change the color of the main menu (Form 330) by adding a new menu item and changing the color of the form 330. However, you will be able to know only the difference between the two DBs when you are in the main menu. So it would be better if you change the name(s) of the company so that they can be easily identified. For instance, suppose Cronus is the company name, then you can keep the live database company name as Cronus and make the test database company's name as Test Cronus.

Question 38: Export Data to Excel .

We just upgraded to client 5.0, SQL 2005 but navision source is still 3.7 (5).

We have new icons to export the data and when we want to export the data to xls, we get following message:

```
"there is no default stylesheet for the program
you are exporting to"
```

Any thoughts or documentation to help us?

A:

First, make sure that your license is updated.

You'll have to add the 5.0 objects for the style sheets to get that working.

Question 39: NAV 5.0 kitting doc

I downloaded a lot of new tech stuff on NAV 5.0 from Partner Source. I am currently looking for tech/training material on the new Kitting module but did not find anything on this module. I have the course 8713 document (Part I & II) but nothing on kitting. Is there anything I missed on the Partner Source? Where I could get such information?

A: This is the first time I hear something about a new Kitting module. There is nothing like this in 5.0 except of the existing Bill of Material. But to run on a brand new kitting module, you have to download and restore the latest database from partner source. In the Download section, filter on NAV 5.0 downloads, you will find "NAV 5.00 North American Pre-Release Database". You just have to restore it and you will be up and running with a brand new Kitting module.

For additional details about the kitting module, visit https://mbs.microsoft.com/partnersource/sales/salestools/prod uctfactsheets/KittingNAVFactSheet.

In NAV NA Pre-release database, you will find "kitting" tab in the following:

1. Item form
2. Quote/SO forms
3. Customer card
4. Kit BOM = Form 25000 (you cannot edit it but can run it). You can find kit BOM in two places in the menu. Proceed to: In Purchase → Inventory & Costing and in the Warehouse → Planning and Execution.

To give you an idea of what kitting is, let us suppose you sell computers and in your inventory you have keyboards, monitors, and cases. But the product you sell is the "2007 Wally Waller brand new super computer 1500Mhz" consisting 1 keyboard, 1 case, and 1 monitor. So when you select that product in the customer order, the system would "use/reserve/consume" the 3 items. It could also be Bathroom kits, Kitchen utensils kits, computers, 3 for 1 offer. Basically the kit itself does not exist. It is a grouping of physical items.

Question 40: Monitoring Navision C/Site DB Space

I am trying to monitor NAVISION with MOM. I am looking for an automation action so I can readout every 1h the free space with a script (vbs or c#).

Can I readout the C/Site DB free space? I know there is an ODBC driver, but is this the right way? Does the database file(s) form c/site db allocate space at the beginning or do they auto grow? What do I need to do next?

A: First go to File → Database → Information and check it there. There you can get all the information and tools that you need.

Autogrow is a part of SQL and not of the Native database. The Native Version does not autogrow. In fact, autogrow for SQL should be used as a safety net and when you need to increase your database you should do it manually. If you let the SQL server decides for you, you will find it to always happen at the most inopportune time.

Question 41: Restoring the Backup

I am restoring the backup xxx.fbk (big one, 2 Gb) and when
indicator reaches 100% there is an error:

```
"File xxx.fbk was not found".
```

Happens in both cases when I restore only application objects
and the whole backup.

What is going on?

A: When you create a backup that has more than 2 GB there is
more than one file *.fbk

Question 42: Navision 3.7 and Vista

Has anybody tried Windows Vista with the Navision 3.7 client?

A few months ago it did not apparently work. Does it work on the released version? Could anyone enlighten me on this?

A: No. It seems like NAV 4, sp3, rollup 1 will be the first version to run on Vista.

Question 43: NAV 4.0 SP3 and Windows RTM Vista

When I try to run the NAV SQL client, I get the following error:

"Internal error: 47-1 (text no. 46-100 does not exist in the .stx file)."

The system works fine on XP clients but we get this problem on our Vista machines.

How can we resolve this issue?

A: The Microsoft Dynamics NAV 4.0 SP3 and Microsoft Office 2007 are compatible immediately. So if you are running on Microsoft Dynamics NAV 4.0 SP3, you can take advantage of Microsoft Office 2007 without upgrading Microsoft Dynamics NAV 4.0 SP3. There is also in the market a Platform Release for Microsoft Dynamics NAV 4.0 SP3 that will make Microsoft Dynamics NAV 4.0 SP3 compatible with Microsoft Windows Vista. The Platform Release enables Microsoft Dynamics NAV 4.0 SP3 customers to run on Microsoft Windows Vista.

However, Microsoft Dynamics NAV 4.0 is not compatible with Microsoft Windows Vista when installed from the released CD or from downloads available from PartnerSource. To be able to run Microsoft Dynamics NAV 4.0 on Microsoft Windows Vista, you need to install Microsoft Dynamics NAV 4.0 SP3 and the platform roll-up update knowledge base article 931841.

To install, you need to make sure to have the following prerequisites in place before you can run Microsoft Dynamics NAV 4.0 SP3 on Vista:

1. Install Microsoft Windows Vista
2. Install Microsoft Dynamics NAV 4.0 SP3
3. Search and Replace the Microsoft Dynamics NAV 4.0 SP3 Platform files with the ones in the updated System Requirements. With this Platform Release, the System Requirements are updated too.

Question 44: Client-Server problem in Vista Business and Navision 4.0

Since I work with Vista Business OS, I cannot connect to the Navision server. There is always a message displayed that I should restart the client, then restart the server and try to connect again.

The server is also available in the network. How can I resolve this problem?

A: Apparently, some users have sent the same problem to Microsoft and this is the official response:

"CAUSE: Windows Vista is still not supported in NAV. Dynamics NAV development is currently working with the latest Release Candidates of Microsoft Office 2007 and Microsoft Windows Vista to ensure compatibility.

RESOLUTION: When Dynamics NAV development has finalized testing, we will announce compatibility with Microsoft Office 2007 and Microsoft Windows Vista. We expect this to be within three month of the release of Microsoft Office 2007 and Microsoft Windows Vista respectively".

Question 45: Navision unstalling

I am trying to install Navision. However, Navision seems to install and then when installation nears completion it uninstalls.

Why is that?

A: You are trying to install Navision on Terminal Server remotely. Terminal Server requires you to login locally to install Navision or any other application.

.

Question 46: Adding or removing granules from a license temporarily

During testing and implementing the software, it would be a great help if one could temporarily add or remove granules to/from a customer license. It helps isolate the functionality from a specific granule and thus demonstrate it to a customer. The same goes for testing. This should be available only for partners of course. Is this possible?

A: You can do this easily enough by setting up roles. Just set up a role that has permission only to the tables you want your customer to test.

Question 47: Potential customer

Our company is contemplating on purchasing Microsoft Navision as an integrated, organization wide solution. I am comfortable with the accounting function within Navision, however, we are very project based and will require very strong project management, payroll (timesheets), and purchasing modules.

Are there any comments for potential customers, significant benefits, things to watch out for, and specific experience with a project management module? Could anyone provide us any help on this matter?

A: Some have done quite a few of these implementations and they did work quite well. But "out of the box", it is very unlikely that Dynamics NAV Jobs will do what you want. The core functionality is there, but you cannot expect such things as tie sheet entry or automated Job billing to be there. You just have to make sure that you buy from a Partner that can show you references where they have implemented the Jobs system, so that you know that they know what they are doing.

The basic Jobs and resource is very basic and a good starting point to build one. You could do several implementations for your client with this functionality. This is the major advantage with NAV. You really need to look for a partner who has experience with implementation of project based solutions. Also, be alert to agree on what is done for the money you want to spend. The focus should be on supporting the primary and some of your secondary business processes and do not try to cover everything. This will cost you a lot and in the end you are not fully satisfied. It is better to start with a good build basis, with not all the needed and wished for functionality. After a while of working with the solution, you will find that your point of view and wishes have changed. Based on this, you can start a second phase in development and will get in the end a better result for you money.

There are a lot of partners who have build solutions for projects and resource. They are not always the major and large partners. But they can do the job nevertheless.

Question 48: Assigning Navision after going out of business

We are using 3.7 and have customized for import/distribution/WMS. We recently went out of business and I am not sure what to do with our software. Is there a market for this or is it possible to assign or sell this license?

A: You can contact Microsoft directly and they will tell you what needs to be done legally. Anyone who buys the license and tries to use it illegally will also end up in great difficulty.

Question 49: Using two printers

I have a number of different printers. Two of these are special; one I use for checks and the other for invoices. How do I tell Navision where to print my checks and invoices?

A: Go to General Ledger-> Setup-> Printer Selections. Enter the report ID for your checks and invoices and where they should be printed.

Question 50: Opening a Folder from a database field

How do you open a folder from a database field? I know there are a lot of "messy" ways to do this.

Im looking for the quick and easy way to do this.

A: Here is a workaround, using a field called "Document folder".

```
txt:
CommonDialogMgmt.OpenFile(Name,"Document
Folder"+'.',1,'',0);

Excel:
CommonDialogMgmt.OpenFile(Name,"Document
Folder"+'.',2,'',0);

Word:
CommonDialogMgmt.OpenFile(Name,"Document
Folder"+'.',1,'',0);

All Files:
CommonDialogMgmt.OpenFile(Name,"Document
Folder"+'.',4,'All Files (*.*)|*.*|All Files
(*.*)|*.*',0);
```

What happens is the common dialog thinks there is a filename because of the added period in the +'.', and nothing comes up in the Filename on the Windows Dialog screen

```
C:\Temp\.
```

No special Automation required

Question 51: Adding a new path to current system path

How can I add a new path string to the current system path?

Using Environ('Path') we are able to retrieve the current system path, but how to add new path string?

Current System Path:

Path = `c:\windows;c:\windows\system32;`

I want to add this path c:\temp;

New system path will be:

Path := `c:\windows;c:\windows\system32;c:\temp;`

A: Use the 'Windows Script Host Object

Model'.FileSystemObject'

```
CreateFolder(NewFolder : Text[100]) : Boolean
IF ISCLEAR(FileSystem) THEN
IF NOT CREATE(FileSystem) THEN
EXIT;

FileSystem.CreateFolder(NewFolder);
```

Question 52: Disaster recovery

I am performing a regular SQL server database backup for my Navision installation. To test my backup for compliance purposes and my own piece of mind, I restored the database to a different SQL server, and then ran some reports as verification that the restoration had worked.

When I try to access the database on the restored server, I receive the error "Your program license permits a maximum of non-demonstration companies. Contact your system manager..." How could I get around this, especially as this would be a similar scenario for Disaster Recovery at a remote site?

A: You get this error because you have not imported your license-file into the SQL database. So all you have to do is to copy your Licensefile FIN.FLF into the folder where you start your Navision then it should work.

Question 53: COM automation and Navision outstreams (BLOB export)

I have done some work in Automations written in C#. Everything works except BLOB´s. I have a BLOB-Field in Navision and would like to export that to my Automation. Here is a code unit example:

```
MyTable.CALCFIELDS(MyTable.Picture);
MyTable.Picture.CREATEINSTREAM(StreamInObj);

COPYSTREAM(StreamOutObj, StreamInObj);
MyAutomationFunc.SendPicture(OuStream);

CLEAR(StreamInObj);
CLEAR(StreamOutObj);
```

I used System.IO.Stream in my C# Interface. On compilation I got some ErrorMessage from Navision:
Automation:=OutStream

Can you point to me the error?

A: You can export the bitmap with an xml port and use a base64 to encode the bitmap into a big text node, then stream the xml file in .net object and decode it there. That's much slower than writing the bitmap to a temp file but it is a sure fire way.

Question 54: Setup checklist

I can't find the setup checklist. Where exactly is it? How do I get there? Could anyone point it for me?

A: There should be no problem if you have 3.7 or earlier. Click on the General Ledger → Setup and then go down the page where you will see the Setup Checklist.

IV. Navision Applications

Question 55: Reports currency format

We got a lot of Navision reports with currency in them. The users like that the currency displays as €3445, 34 and not 3445, 34. What is the best way to do this? What do I do next?

A: You can try the format property or you can add something as '€ ' + recSalesHeader.Amount in your sourceexpression. Or you can add another label in front.

Question 56: Purchase order archive

I have a client that would like to use the archive capabilities of Navision. I cannot seem to figure out what granules they would need to use it. They currently have all the purchasing options, with the exception of discounting.

A: You could try Granule ID 5160 - CRM - Interaction/Document Management.

Question 57: MIS postings in analysis by dimension

I wanted to see if anybody else had an issue with postings missing from an analysis by dimension. I have issues where a journal entry will post but could not be captured in the Analysis by Dimension. It happens somewhat on a regular basis but there seems to be no trend in the accounts being used or the analysis itself. I am just wondering if anybody else came across this and if there are any fixes required. Do you have any ideas on how to approach this issue?

A: First, have you made sure that your Analysis View is updated. If not, you have to check the box 'Update on Posting' and then you will need to manually update it if you want to see the posting immediately. To manually update your Analysis View, go into the Analysis View Card and click the button on the bottom called update. Also, check your Date Compression. If it is set to 'Day', then your Analysis View will update each day.

Question 58: Filtering

I want to filter the customer list when creating sales invoice, that is, when I enter the first character in customer name text box, the customer list displays and filters according from the sales invoice customer name text box.

A: You could just look up on the 'Sell-to Customer No.' as normal and use the built-in and add the 'You Type' functionality.

Question 59: Removing invoices from suggested payment list

I had an invoice posted to a wrong vendor number. I issued a credit memo to the invoice to remove the invoice from the vendor. The vendor now has a zero account balance, but both entries appear on the suggested payment list. How do I remove these entries from the suggested payment list?

A: You have to check the Vendor Ledger entries for the remaining amount column and see if it says zero. Then look at other column Open, which should not have a check mark on these entries. If there is a check mark in the Open column of these entries, then you might have to apply the documents to each other again.

Question 60: Opening invoice in MS Word

I want to print an invoice in a Word document from NAV4.0. How can I use the Automation Server in Navision and open the Word document?

A: To get an idea of how it works, you have to check the Sales & Marketing - Contacts, which creates a Word document in NAV when you create an interaction for a contact.

Question 61: Navision 3.7 copy and 'paste' does not work

We recently noticed that when we copy information from a table in Navision and try to paste it in Excel, not all the data is brought over. We never noticed this happening in 2.6.

It has happened on 2 of our company machines and on 1 of our VAR machines. It has happened in both forms and object designer tables. It happens on more than one table data. It is not the filters. I was running a comparison of data and was viewing the missing data.

The problem I experienced was that it did not copy all the records and a few of the records it copied were pasted multiple times on the same row in excel - in essence adding additional columns to excel. It also skipped past some records and did not include them in the paste. This has just come to light and it is so bad that we cannot use the copy paste function from Navision to another program. Our VAR does not know what is causing this.

What is causing this and how we can fix it?

A: Copying from NAV and pasting to Excel is pretty straight forward. When copying large amount of data it takes a while for Windows to put it on the clipboard. You can check the clipboard for data before pasting it to excel.

For further readings on other ways of getting data into excel, visit the following URLs:

Category: General downloads

Description: Export data from any table directly to Excel with greater ease and flexibility! Only basic report skills are required to implement the Excel Template Based Exporter (ETBE).

More powerful than a dataport:
Dataports rely on hardcoding the order of field data in the Field Designer. The ETBE isn't constrained to one layout. Just create a

new Excel file with the fields needed in the first row and the ETBE does the rest. Use the same report object with different template files to export table data in any field combination. All without ever writing a field name in the code!

Empower your users to customize their own excel templates. Give them the ability to:
- select the fields THEY want to see
- arrange the fields in any order
- rename what the fields are called in the export file
- pre-design excel file (print settings, format, color, etc)
- filter and so rt data just as any basic report has to offer
- include extra data from associated tables (some code required)

ETBE IS SECURE: since ETBE uses the basic report objects of Navision, users only have access to the tables you set them up to have (all while maintaining their predefined permissions).

How to use:
Just create a basic report with one dataitem. Then, add the three public function calls to the included Codeunit. The example report included demonstrates how to:
1. Initialize codeunit in OnPreDataItem
2. Export data for each record in OnAfterGetRecord
3. Save the final export in the OnPostRecord
(the easiest way is to save the included excel template directly to C:\)

Learn Excel Automation Here:
If you are new to Excel Automation, I encourage you to take a look at the code. The comment-filled codeunit provides a great overview of what is needed to make an excel export happen.

I have found this to be a very helpful tool. I originally designed it for a specific task but then later came to recognize it as a more general multi-purpose module. I am glad to take the time to package it up and be able to share it with others.

Question 62: Availability of system generated field for all tables

To migrate the data from a legacy system to NAV, I have to import the data from the flat file (Excel sheet) to the NAV Database. While importing the data into NAV, would the system generate any new values in any table?

A: If you using a dataport, you can import the data as long as you have the primary key values of the table filled in. I do not think there is any new data generated unless there is code to generate it.

Question 63: Calculating multiple VAT in purchase journal

While getting the invoice from a vendor, there are some different products with different VAT percentage available. In the Purchase Journal, how could we calculate and enter multiple VAT for that invoice? Is it possible?

A: You can not do that in Purchase Journals but you can do that in Purchase Invoice/Order. You can select different products with different VAT percentages on the different lines of the Purchase Invoice.

Question 64: Building sales portal

We have a customer who plans to buy Microsoft Navision 4.0. He would like that his Field Sales representatives be able to view the inventory on hand through the web. What is the possibility of doing it in Navision?

A: You can purchase the employee portal. But you can also create web pages via ASP that will provide what you are looking for. This is assuming that the ODBC driver and you can host the web site from within your network to have access to the Navision Server. Another way is to have a web based solution which has real-time integration with NAV. It is a B2B / B2C solution.

Question 65: Aging inventory

Is anyone aware of a standard report or other means by which we could determine the age of inventory? We are instructed to move inventory off our manufacturing floor if it is over 30 days old regardless of the type (finished goods, WIP, raw materials, etc.). Could somebody explain how we could do it?

A: For information about your problem, try reading Report No. 5807 for Item Age Composition – Quantity and Report 5808 for Item Age Composition – Value. You could try giving filters as per your requirement. Moreover, you could also look at Report #10146 on Item Turnover.

Question 66: Formatting

I want to open a URL with parameters and made the following code:

hyperlink ('www.xxxx.dk/admin/yyyy.asp?Amount=%1' , rec.amount);

I parsed the amount from a sales line to the URL (%1) but every time I do it, the results look like this:
www.xxxx.dk/admin/yyyy.asp?Amount=0

How could I convert the amount to a string? The amount field is like this: 12.334,77.

A: You could try this code:

HYPERLINK(STRSUBSTNO('www.xxxx.dk/admin/yyyy.asp?Amount=%1',rec.Amount));

Question 67: Transaction number

It would be nice to have a unique transaction number in all ledger entry tables. This field should uniquely identify the ledger entries that were created in a single transaction. For example, every time F11 is executed. Is this possible?

A: The 'Transaction No.' field is already in most Ledger Entry tables and it solves the same purpose. You could check the field in the G/L Entry, Customer and Vendor Ledger Entry tables, etc.

You could also try the "Job Ledger Entry" and the "Item Ledger Entry". Moreover, this is a relational database, so you so not have to have all information in one table.

Question 68: WIP reports

Is there any report that can tell me exactly what jobs are in the WIP account at the end of a period or the 'Over billing' account?

A: This report is not available for 'Jobs' but it would be fairly easy one to be created by a partner.

Question 69: Year end closing

I need to close the year but I am having trouble doing it, ending up posting transactions twice and thus have to undo and then redo it. The consultant sent me a book containing lots of steps that I should do to close the year. But I just wanted some simple step by step instructions. If I follow the book sent to me, I am afraid I would end up with a mess again.

Moreover, I need to a prior year adjustment and I also do not know how. I looked it up in the Help section and it said to click the prior year entry column, bit I do not have that column.

Is there a better way to do this right?

A: I am afraid that there is no "easy way" to solve this issue.

There are three steps involved in the Annual closing operation.

1. Close the Fiscal Year

When you select to close the year, the program automatically selects the oldest year open. Once you have confirmed that you wish to close the year, the closed and the date locked fields of all periods in that fiscal year will be updated and a check-mark will be displayed. This check-mark cannot be removed. The period lengths of the closed periods can not be changed as well.

When you close the fiscal year, the program will lock the period-length, but it will not block against entering and posting transactions to those closed periods. This can be done from General Ledger|Periodic Activities-Fiscal Year-Accounting Periods window.

2. Run the Close Income Statement process

The batch job processes all G/L accounts of the Income Statement type and creates entries that cancel out their respective balances. These closing entries are placed in a journal, in which you must specify a balancing account in the balance sheet before posting. This can be done under General Ledger|Periodic Activities-Fiscal Year-Close Income Statement window.

3. Post the Closed Income Statement journal

When the journal is posted, an entry is posted to each income statement account so that its balance becomes zero and an opposite amount is transferred to the balance sheet. You must post the journal yourself unless you are posting additional reporting currency. If you are posting an additional reporting currency, the program will automatically post the journal because this guarantees the correct posting of rounding differences. This can be done under General Ledger|General Journals.

The date on the lines that the batch job inserts in the journal will always be a closing date for the fiscal year. The closing date is a fictitious date between the last day of the old fiscal year and the first day of the new year. It is designated as a closing date by having the format Cmm/dd/yy. The advantage of this format is to maintain correct balances for the ordinary dates of the fiscal year.

Question 70: Identifying and purging inactive customers

Our customer database continuously grows and I can't figure out a good way to identify and then delete customers who have been active for some period of time only. For instance, I would like to delete all those customers who have not ordered anything in the past two years.

Is there a report or function that would be helpful to use?

I can print out a list of those who have ordered over a period of time, but not a list of inactive customers. We use Navision 4.0.

A: One idea is to create a flowfield on the Posting date of the Customer Ledger Entries. Below are the sample steps on how to go about it.

1. In the Customer Table, add a field Called "Last Invoice Date" = Type Date
2. In the properties of that field, you make its type flowfield
3. In the CalcFormula, you can put
Max("Cust. Ledger Entry"."Posting Date" WHERE (Document Type=FILTER(Invoice),Customer No.=FIELD(No.)))

The 'Max' should give you the largest date. It filters only Invoices and it is Customer specific. So it should only show the date of the last invoice for that customer. Now, add the new field to the customer card and you can then filter on this date. You can make it for both Invoice and Credit Memos too.

Question 71: Downloading journal entries

I am trying to obtain a listing of who can initiate, approve, and post journal entries. I need the complete list of Journal entries from 2006. Is there a canned report that already exists or is there a method (SQL query) to pull this information from the SQL database?

A: If you are talking about posted journal lines, you can create a report from the G/L entry table and filter on source code GENJNL and other parameters as required, like the date filter etc.

Question 72: Closing sales orders

We are in the contract manufacturing business and thus we would like to keep a history of the sales orders that are cancelled to be able to rate the customer or item performance. We often have customers that cancel their purchase orders after we have already created sales orders and often production orders too. We would like to be able to "close" a sales order that has been cancelled by the customer or the shipped quantity is equal to the demand quantity. Is there any way to change the Sales Order "status" to cancel (if cancelled by the customer) or "closed" if we have satisfied the demand on the order and yet retain the order for historical reporting? If we could look every 6 or 12 months at the number of sales orders that were cancelled by customer it may allow us to make more informed decisions about the future of those customers. Could anyone advice us?

A: If you have a developer's license and just looking for a way to mark these sales orders so you can create a report or just be able to filter on them, then you can do the following: First, create a new field on the sales header table called "Canceled Order" type Boolean and then add it to the header. You can check the box off every time an order is cancelled. This field can be used to filter on cancelled orders only. Another way is to create a lookup on the customer card where on a click, it would list all the canceled orders for that customer.

A similar system could be made for canceling Posted Sales Invoices. You could make a Boolean field on the Sales Invoice Header table called Invoice Cancelled and a report that can toggle the field. You could need this for billing purposes. Generally, if an invoice is cancelled (i.e., credited) you do not want to send the Invoice to the customer.

Question 73: Error 1355 in Module 19

I am getting an error message while running a report (related to item ledger entries and production order) as "Internal error 1355 in module 19". What is the impact or cause of this error message? How do you explain this error?

A: There's not much information about this error. But here are some points regarding this error that could help you understand it.

1. You will get the error message when a particular piece of code in the database manager is called twice that's probably from two different processes.
2. The DBM is not reentrant. The machine is probably slow because there are no more resources. The solution is to reboot regularly.
3. The error has been noticed when applying a filter on a field that does not belong to the key. The filter will be saved to the zup file. Removing this file should solve this problem, or create a new key.
4. The CPU stack is full.

A possible solution is to optimize all tables in the database.

Question 74: Posting invoices problem

We run NAV 3.70 and are having some difficulties with some invoices that do not post or delete in sales and receivables. This is the error message:

"Sales Invoice Header number 15523 already exists."

The invoice doesn't even show up on the computer that is having the problem.

How can we fix this?

A: You could try to look at the "Posting No." field in Sales Header table. Probably, the posted invoice "15523" all ready exists. You can try to delete the value in that field, If that don't help, someone is messing with your posting invoice series, so go to the posting invoice series and modify the last used number.

If you have the proper license, go to object designer (SHIFT + F12), find table 36, press 'RUN', find the header row of problem record, and delete value in "Posting no." field. After that you should be able to post or delete that sales header number. If you don't have license permission to do that, you should contact your Navision partner and ask her to repair your problem.

In other words, you can add the Posting No. field to your sales header so you can see it and change it. It's not on the form by default, but you can add it though. Once visible, you can now delete it. This also happens when a sales order which is going to be invoiced is canceled in the middle of posting. The Posting No. gets filled but not cleared when you cancel or if the pc crashes, etc.

Question 75: Invoice issue: "Sell to Cus #"

On one of our machines we are not able to change the sell-to customer no. in an invoice. It continuously comes up with the same customer. This does not happen on any of the other machines. We run NAV 3.70.

Could somebody explain to us this problem or what to do next?

A: You should delete that machines fin.zup file and try again. Even if you delete it, it will be recreated the next time you login. Also, it is a hidden file so make sure you make hidden files visible.

You could also try to use an id=something here in the shortcut to Navision. This will ensure that you get a new and fresh .zup file if there are some problems with that. You should be able to find a something.zup after you have ended the Navision session, if not there is something wrong.

Also, check that there are no responsibility center settings which are blocking the usage of that customer.

Question 76: Applying cash

I have a client in the electrical industry that deals with a large group of wholesalers. Sales orders come in from individual branches (i.e., each branch needs to be a customer and may have its own pricing) but the invoice goes to a "district" office (i.e. the "Bill-to" customer). The problem arises in that a statement is issued to a head office (i.e., the one above the district offices) and the payment comes in from the head office. This makes cash allocation very difficult to apply.

Is there a functional solution possible?

A: You could assign all the related accounts as parent-child relationships. When you go to apply a payment, you apply it to the head office and all the open entries for the related accounts allow you to pay them.

You can define the relationship by either using Chain Name or the Bill-to-Account No. You can do either way if you want all the billings from one or many separate customers to all go to one account. You can set them all with the head offices Bill-to number. Then all the bills will appear there.

There is a functionality called Parent Customer Number, which is part of a third party add-on for A/R called Fast Cash back in ver 3.10. It could have been added already to the newer versions. By filling in the same Parent Customer No. in as many accounts as you wish, when you enter a payment you will get all the open entries. All the entries from all the customers that have been linked together by the Parent Customer No. appear.

Question 77: Inventory quantity by location

What tables and fields and calculations does Navision use to display the "Inventory" value on the Item card? I want to write a report that displays all stocks in a location. I have gone through some of the tables trying to find one that has a field of location, when looking in Item related tables, or a field for item when looking in Location/warehouse related tables, and I can't find any. I figured there would be something that shows items going in and out of a location and then you could filter on the item and location of that table and the SUM the value field (+ and - together should equal the balance).

How do I fix this?

A: On the Item ledger Entry table, you can filter on the card to see the quantity on each location and/or you can modify and/or add another qoh field for each location by adjusting the flowfield.

If you wanted to create a report - I would use the Item Ledger Entry Table. If you just wanted to see the Qty on hand of a location you can go to the item card and hit Ctrl-F7 which will bring you to the item flowfilter. Here you can set the filter for the location you are interested in. All the item info now showing on the card is for that location only. Another way depending on if you have just a few locations is simply create a new quantity on hand field for each location because many times you'll see that you forgot change the flowfilter filter or forget to even add it. also it disappears if someone alters the card and complies it. You wouldn't even know. Anyway - by going to the item table you create a new field "QOH-Location1" or whatever suits you - Type Decimal. Field Class-Flowfield now by viewing the CalcFormula of the original quantity on hand field (Field 68). You copy & paste it into your new field then drill into the formula and add an additional filter for that location. Add the new field it to your item card and you're done. Now you can see the total quantity on hand and a new quantity in location1. You can do as many as you like. Just note this is an ok method for few locations if you have say less than 10. More than that, then it can get a bit messy. Also note that you can add the location filter to the Inventory valuation report to find out what's on hand in the different locations.

Question 78: Inventory value <> 0 when item quantity = 0

We have an ongoing problem with Navision. Most of our items are purchased, and then sold in 1 to four (4) lots. However, often, we end up with a remaining quantity of 0, but with an inventory value not equal to $0. In fact today, I have 38 items that all have a quantity of 0, but the combined inventory value is equal to >$72K.

I can find no way to "write off" these values. I've tried adding material, selling material, etc. My local Navision support company has a fix where they "zap" my records.

In most systems, I can directly write to the inventory sub-ledger which would allow me to credit the item and debit COGS. My auditors and bankers are screaming. How do I make this right?

A: This can occur when some entries have not been invoiced and expected cost varies between positive (purchases) and negative (sales) entries. If you are running the valuation report for a prior date, this issue can occur if 'Adjust Cost' have posted entries with dates beyond the valuation date that apply to entries included in the valuation. Check for this and correct the problem at hand.

Question 79: Changing Properties during runtime

Which of the following properties you can change during runtime? why?

a) visible

b) vertglue

c) sourceExpr

A: "Visible" because when runtime we can show column or hide column that means you can make it visible or not visible

Question 80: Mixing text and expression in a text box

I am using the report designer in Navision 4. Does anyone know how to display the content of a table-field and some text in the same text box? Could anyone provide me the steps on how to do this?

A: You can use the STRSUBSTNO command:

e.g. STRSUBSTNO('Total for Product Group Code %1',Item."Product Group Code")

You can either place the command directly in the SourceExpr property of a text box or assign the result to a text variable and use that as the source expression. You can use as many substitutions as you need, i.e. %2 %3 %4.

Question 81: Line amount before discount

Is it possible to create a field in the invoice report that will represent the net amount of the item before having the discount? Let's say:

quantity:1
unit price:100
line amount before discount:100
discount:10%
line amount:90

A: You can do it in two ways. First is to create a variable called LineAmtBeforeDisc and then you can calculate it by either one of the following:

LineAmtBeforeDisc := Quantity * "Unit Price";
or
LineAmtBeforeDisc := "Amount Including Tax" + "Line Discount Amount";

But it is recommended that you use LineAmtBeforeDisc := Quantity * "Unit Price"; since the other way is specific to the US version. Amount Includes tax and is also a total of invoice and not line specific where the line amount before discount has to be line specific. Hence, you can go with LineAmtBeforeDisc := Quantity * "Unit Price";

Question 82: G/L post and print Navision 3.70 client

The Post and Print feature seems only to Post and NOT Print. It does work though in other modules i.e., Inventory Journal. I am not sure where to start looking for issues. There is nothing in the Event Logs. The Client uses XP Pro SP2 that is configured to use network printers.

How can this be resolved?

A: Chances are that the user printed a register using the G/L Register report (10019 in the US database), leaving a filter behind that combined with the Register No. filter that the posting routine passes, give a result of zero records. Most often it is used to print all transactions for a date range or such.

The easiest way to fix this is to go into design mode on the report and then save it, which will reset the zup-file settings for all users. If this solves it, then copy the report and add the new report to the menus instead of the default one.

Question 83: Modifying sales invoice header

I've modified the Sales Invoice Header table (112) to include a number of new fields, which are transferred from the Sales Header table (36) when the Sale is posted. I need to be able to update these new fields after the Sale has been posted. However, trying to do so gives the message error "You do not have permission to modify records in the Sales Invoice Header table."

I only want to modify the fields I've added to the table, not the existing ones. I've looked at the Sales Invoice Printed codeunit (315) but I can find no way to use its permissions on another codeunit to enable editing - I still get the same error.

Can someone suggest where I might be going wrong? I'll admit my understanding of Navision's use of Permissions isn't my strong point. Could anyone help?

A: If you look at codeunit 391 Shipment Header – Edit, you will find the following:

SalesInvoiceHeaderEdit ← On this trigger you need to add SalesInvoiceHeader2."YourField" := SalesInvoiceHeader."YourField";

The Sales Invoice Header table is a protected table, which users cannot make changes to. All posted document and ledger tables are protected as you do not want users to make changes to posted data, which would compromise the integrity of the system. The only way for a customer to get access to protected tables is to buy the Solution Developer granule.

If the customer bought the Sales Invoicing granule they receive indirect permissions for the posted sales document tables which you will see as lower case permissions on the customer's license configuration file (rimd).

If the customer has direct permissions to a table this will show with upper case letters (RIMD). That a customer has indirect permissions to a table means that they cannot change the data in the table directly, but you can however; give as an example a codeunit permissions to change the data in the table. If you look at for example codeunit 80 – Sales-Post you will see that this codeunit has permissions to Insert, Modify, and Delete in table 112 – Sales Invoice Header, which means that even though the customer's license doesn't give the customer permissions to directly insert and modify records in the Sales Invoice Header table codeunit 80 will be able to insert and modify records into the table when a sales invoice is posted.

You can use this functionality to modify fields on the Posted Sales Invoice form as well and this has already been done on the Posted Sales Shipment form where you can change the Package Tracking No, Shipping Agent Code, and Shipping Agent Service Code fields. This is done by having a codeunit make the changes and by giving this codeunit permission to the Sales Shipment Header table. If you want your customer to be able to modify fields on the Posted Sales Invoice form you can create functionality similar to what has been done for the Posted Sales Shipment form. You can use the same codeunit as is used on the Posted Sales Shipment form, codeunit 391 – Shipment Header - Edit, and add a new function to this codeunit where you change the fields in the Sales Invoice Header table and give the codeunit permissions for the Sales Invoice Header table as well or you can create a new codeunit for this functionality. The codeunit is called from the OnModifyRecord trigger on the Posted Sales Shipment form.

If you want more information about the Application Builder granule you can find it in KB article 878370.

"Protected tables" refers to those tables that can only be written to by objects with special permissions set. These tables are generally the Ledger Entry tables and the Register tables, and certain history tables. The objects that have permission to update these tables (posting routines and adjustment routines for example) can only be created or modified by users who have the Solution Developer granule.

With the Application Builder Granule you can only modify tables that are not protected tables. The Sales Invoice Header table is a protected table (history table).

Question 84: Editable Field on a Non-Editable Form

How do you setup an editable field on a non-editable form?

A:

In the OnAfterGetCurrRecord on the form there is the following code:

```
CODE: CurrForm.EDITABLE(status = status::open);
```

So if status is released the form is non-editable.

But 1 field still has to be editable...

In the OnActivate of the field I put:

```
CODE: CurrForm.EDITABLE(TRUE);
```

In the OnDeActivate of the field I put:

```
CODE: CurrForm.EDITABLE(status = status::open);
```

V. Navision Reports & Table Formats

Question 85: Check Stub on top

I would like to reformat the existing Check in Nav 5.0 so that it will have the check stub to print on top.

I have tried to rearrange the fields and move it on top.
I have tried adding some other sections and I am not successful.

Please advise.

A: There are standard reports

10401 Check (Stub/Stub/Check)
10411 Check (Stub/Check/Stub).

Question 86: Displaying Contents of a Table-Field

I am using the report designer in Navision 4. Does anyone know how to display the content of a table-field and some text in the same text box?

A: You can use the STRSUBSTNO command, e.g., STRSUBSTNO('Total for Product Group Code %1',Item."Product Group Code");

You can either place the command directly in the SourceExpr property of a text box or assign the result to a text variable and use that as the source expression.

You can use as many substitutions as you need, i.e., %2 %3 %4

Question 87: OptionCaption on an option type field from a table

Is it possible to have OptionCaption and/or OptionCaptionML from an Option Type Field of a Table by a SQL query? I need this to do an export to a BI database. I have only values (0, 1, 2, 3, 4, 5, 6, and 7) but not their Captions.

How do I go about this?

A: You could try to use the "FORMAT"-command. It is possible to do that because the OptionString of a field is stored in the SQL database.

Question 88: Drawing a line on a report

I'd like to use a code to draw a line below a section on a report only when the Status field equals active. I am new to CA/L programming but not to programming.

Is there more information on this?

A: You will need to create a section in your report containing the horizontal line, and following code in the OnPreSection-trigger of this section:

Currreport.SHOWOUTPUT (Status = Status::Active);

This way, the section is only printed, when the Status field is Active.

Moreover, if you need to add a horizontal line, you can add a "Shape" using the tool bar and look for the shapes properties and set it to horizontal line and then stretch the field the length of the report.

Question 89: Footer question

The group footers do not show when I print a report, i.e., the footers including labels and text boxes. I expect them to show-up right after the body.

What is wrong here and how could this be resolved?

A: Just make sure that the field(s) you want to group are specified in the GroupTotalFields property of the DataItem in question AND that these field(s) are included in a key specified in the DataItemTableView property. The problem is with the GroupTotalFields property.

Question 90: Editable property

Can any one explain the influence of the editable property of a field in the table? Can we change or edit the data in the field whose editable property is set to "no". If yes, how we can change/edit it?

What are the processes involved on how to do this?

A: If editable is set to "no", then you can not change it. Even if you set it to "yes", it still depend on the table permissions whether you can change it. For example, you can set everything to editable on a sales invoice but you probably do not have permission to change it. It is just like the ledger entry table.

For fields, use this property to make a field for display only. For controls, if the Editable setting for the container that contains this control is set to No, that setting overrides what you enter here.
If a form has Editable set to No, then the controls on the form will not be editable, even if their (individual) Editable properties are set to Yes. This property can be set dynamically by using the UPDATEEDITABLE function in the OnBeforeInput trigger of the control.

If you set the editable property to NO for a field in a table, you can still modify the data in it using the C/AL code (triggers or code unit). The editable-property is used when a) you put the field on a form, or b) you run the table using the Object Designer.

So, if a field has the Editable-property set to "No", you cannot enter a value in this field when you run the table, but you can change the value using C/AL:

recVar."My Field" := 'value of field';
recVar.MODIFY;

Question 91: Limitations on part storage

I am new to Navision (now Dynamics NAV) and exploring the possibilities of developing it for our company, a wholesale manufacturer of security doors and screens. I have read a lot on the program but I would like to know if there is a limitation on part storage. Another program that I am comparing it to has a very limited part storage of up to only 3,000 parts but we need a minimum of 50,000.

How do I resolve this issue?

A: The item-table where you will store your parts has a unique key field "No." which is a Code-field with length 20. In this field, you can store characters and numbers. So there should be no problem to have more than 50,000 items stored in this table.

Question 92: Exporting table reference information using dataport

I started working on something in Navision 4 SP3 Update 1 and will work on it later in SQL 2005 based. The first part of the assignment is to write a dataport that is going to get the following out of Navision.

- 'Table Name'
- 'Table ID'
- 'Field Name'
- 'Field ID'

And stick it all in a tab delimited file on the users desktop. It sounds easy but when I sat down to actually do it, I could not figure out how to go about it. I am new to Navision and I have been working with it off and on for about five months now.

How do I go about this?

A: There is a system table called 'Field'. It should contain the data you are looking for.

Question 93: Data Import

I have a csv file placed on http://www.Vendor.com/stocklist.csv.
Is it possible to import directly into Navision database from a
http without saving the file somewhere on our file system first?

A: You cannot directly import into Navision from the http
without saving the file on your file system first but it can be
automated.

However, you can "download" the mentioned file to your PC.
You can use the ftp component to copy the file from that website
to your desktop. Then use XML-port to import it in a non-
standard table. If you can't download the file by ftp, there should
be a web service running. If so you can ask that file by http-
request.

Question 94: Importing MS Access database in Navision 4

Can somebody guide me on how to access a "MS Access"
database in Navision 4.

A: The best way that you can do this is to use C/ODBC or
C/Front.

Question 95: Copying and pasting from Navision to Excel

We are trying to copy and paste the journal line with few thousand records into Excel. However, this feature seems to have a bit of problem as there is always some missing lines in the Excel file. How could I overcome this problem?

Our user will usually copy the records in Navision and do some manipulation in Excel. We can't afford to design a dataport or export to excel functions for them as different user will have their own selected fields to be exported out.

Is there an easier way to go about this?

A: For general downloads, you can follow these guidelines below:

Description: Import data from Excel to any table in just 3 clicks is now possible!

Universal Excel Importer allows you to import data directly from Excel file to any table. Select Excel file, then select worksheet, then select fields and you're done!

UEI has many extra options available. Most of the options are selectable by user (1), or settable inside Excel file (2), or can be predefined as a parameter passed to import function(3).

The options are:

- selection whether to import new records, update existing ones, or do both actions (1)(3)
- predefinition destination table number (1)(2)(3)
- individual selection of fields to import (1)(2)
- define mapping from Excel column to Table Field (1)(2)
- put a filter to column numbers which user can choose to import (3)
- individually select fields on which VALIDATE will be launched (1)(2)(3)

- selection whether to use OnInsert/OnValidate triggers (1)(3)
- matching of fields by Field No, Field Name or Field Caption in working language (3)

User can be also prevented from changing any of above option.

UEI does not modify any standard table.

UEI assumes that header is placed in first non-empty row. It skips empty rows between data, and skips non empty rows if the data is placed in columns not selected to import

UEI by default tries to match names in Excel header row to field captions, so easiest way to prepare Excel template to import is:

1. open destination table (directly or on some form)
2. select one row
3. copy and paste to Excel
4. delete copied data but leave header row
5. delete unnecessary columns or rename names in header
6. fill desired data in appropriate columns.

All fields which are parts of primary key of destination table have to be included in Excel.

To define destination table inside Excel put table:tableNo in A1 cell (no spaces!). That case Importer starts to search for header from row 2.

To define individually which on columns launch VALIDATE simply bold the header field, and put 128 in option passed to Import function. By default all fields are VALIDATEd

New in version 1.1:

- error in Update mode removed (occurring in some cases when updating records with option data type fields in primary key)

- default insertion mode changed - now importing to journals is possible in only one step

- added Delayed Insert option (1)(3) – record will not be inserted until all fields are filled from Excel.

- added possibility of specifying where the data starts inside Excel file (2)(3) - put header:headerRowNo in configuration row and Importer will skip all rows until selected row number, and then will start to search for table header from here. Useful for putting some comments, or any oth er non imported data, at the beginning of Excel file.

Configuration row – it is first non-empty row in Excel file containing at least one parameter definition in any cell. If found Importer will search for table header from next row or from row number specified in parameters.

Valid parameters in version 1.1 are:
header:headerRowNo
table:tableNo

Question 96: Security and domain groups

We are implementing Navision with a partner for a customer. For ease of use, we only want to add a user to a domain group. The partner says that we also need to add the windows users to the SQL-server and then start the Navision synchronization. Is this true? Isn't it there is a way where Navision gets the usernames from the domain group?

A: You have two different user types in Navision - database and windows users. It sounds like that you would like to use Windows users and you still need to add these in Navision and then synchronize with the SQL server. But you don't need to add these users in SQL.

The reason for this is that the NAV application controls the access level within the application. Therefore you will need to setup Windows users within the application. If you go the other route and used database users, you would have to add these in the SQL as well.

Thus, it would be better to use the Windows users, since when using this; the end user will not have to remember an additional setup of logins.

Question 97: Creating order records automatically

I am relatively new to MS Dynamics NAV, and am just looking for some direction on how to do the following:

We have a tab delimited file from a supplier which contains order information, and we would like to load these orders into our NAV system rather than re-keying them. What are the requirements and methods used to do this type of customization or implementation?

How can I fix this?

A: You can create a dataport to import the records. Moreover, the application designer's guide, which is located on the NAV Product CD, has a whole chapter on creating and using dataports.

If you know C/SIDE coding, you have to design a Dataport for this and depending on whether you need this file imported in Purchase Journal or Purchase document (header and detail) this should not take more then 3-4 hours at the maximum.

If the business process is to manually import the files, then use Dataports. But if you plan on automating the process and having it executed by an Application Server, then you will need to avoid Dataports and can use either a Report or Codeunit to do the same thing. You will however need to write extra codes to manage the file handling.

VI. Navision Software Installation, Upgrades, and Tools

Question 98: Installation of Navision 2.6

My client has a valid license for 5 concurrent users for Navision 2.6B that is presently installed on a NT Server. A server upgrade has been approved to Windows 2000 Server with SP4. Though there is a valid license, there is no copy of the software. Inside the Navision software on the Windows NT system, there seems to be a copy of the server software and the financial client's software. Can I use this to install into Windows 2000 Server or do I am required to use the full application CD. If the application CD is lost and granting that the client has the license file and receipt for payment since 2000, how can one obtain another copy of this application so that the installation can be done.

The goal is to install a fresh copy on the new Windows 2000 Server and to restore the full backup made from the copy on the Windows NT server, which we are retiring.

How can I accomplish this?

A: If you are saying that somebody has made a copy of the server and client folders from the CD, then that is all that you need. Your reseller should be able to provide a CD. To restore the backup, just stop the service, copy the database to the new server and install the new service pointing to that data.

Assuming that the old server is "not" used for any other purpose, then its IP address can be changed. You can do the installation using the wizard if you wish, but it would be much better to do it manually so that you would have control. This method allows you to do a DOS copy of the database parts to a different server with a different path without the need to do a Navision backup and restore. (Navision uses the phrase "servername". This is NOT the same as the Windows server name. The Navision "servername" is the name of the SERVICE that you are installing and can be different to the Windows server name.)

1. Make a Navision backup somewhere safe.
2. Make a note of the Navision service name.

3. Make a note of the Navision servers IP address, services and hosts file entries.
4. Stop the Navision service.
5. Copy of the database parts onto the new server (not a Navision backup and restore).
6. Change the IP address of the old server so it doesn't clash with the new one.
7. Edit the new servers SERVICE and HOSTS file as required.
8. Install Navision, call the service FRED and accept the defaults for cache etc, you are going to uninstall this service anyway. Do not point this service at the database parts; select the option to do it later.
9. Don't forget to install the license file (or just copy it across from the old server).
10. Go to the command prompt and go to the Navision folder. Type the following to uninstall the service that was created at installation: "server servername=fred, unistallasservice"
11. As a precaution, delete the dbms.zup file if there is one. Then install the new service using the same service name used on the old server (change the values as required).

    server servername=INSERTSEVICENAME,
    database=e:\part1.fdb+f:\part2.fdb+g:\part3.fdb,
cache=850000,
    commitcache=yes, installasservice

12. Start the service and you are done. Because you have kept the service name and IP address the same as the old one, you do not need to make any changes to your client PCs.

Always use this manual method to install Navision because you can usually copy the database parts to another server with different drive letters for the database path. One thing to watch out for is setting the cache too high. If you do this then the service will not start. You will have to experiment.
Note that the instructions above only apply to the Native version, not the SQL version. The SERVICES and HOSTS file are located at c:\windows\system32\drivers \etc\ and you will need to edit them.

You can name the Navision service whatever you like, say NAVTEST1 . You can then have NAVTEST1 listening on the TCP

port of your choice. To do this, edit the SERVICES file and go to
the bottom. Add the following line and save it (change the name
to the same as you Navision service name).

navtest1   60000/tcp   #Navision Test1 Database

The service NAVTEST1 will now accept connections on port
60000. (On a test server you can have multiple databases
running by naming the next service something else like
NAVTEST2 and using another port number, say 60001). The
HOSTS file would have the following (change the IP address to
your servers one).

192.168.1.2   navtest1

Your clients will need to be configured so that they can connect
to NAVTEST1 on TCP port 60000. How you do that depends on
your network and preferences.

On the clients, you can add 192.168.1.2 navtest1 to the HOSTS of
each PC. But you can also do it through WINS/DNS, after all it
only needs to resolve 192.168.1.2 to the hostname navtest1 so it's
your choice on method. You can then drop an icon on to the
desktop like this:

"C:\Program Files\Navision Client 40\fin.exe"
servername=navtest1:60000, id=navtest1, objectcache=70000,
nettype=tcp

This means that you don't need to edit the SERVICES file on
each client PC. It also creates a ZUP file that is named the same
as the service name (useful on multiple installs of the client).
The object cache does as its name suggests. Navision 4 is around
67Mb(?) and the nettype is obviously TCP.

Question 99: Migration tool kits

I'm trying to migrate the database from Navision 2.6 SG to
Navision 4.0 SP3, but the migration tools provided by Microsoft
are not designed for Navision 2.6 SG. Can you please kindly
provide me the migration tools to migrate from Navision 2.6 SG
to Navision 4.0 SP3?

A: You should be aware of all the changes made in the versions
between 2.60 and 4.0 that may impact your data. For that
reason, Microsoft only provides upgrade tools from a specific
version into a next one (for example from 3.70 to 4.0, no
cumulative tools). You will have to run the several previous
upgrade tools to get your data into the most recent version:
260->3.01->3.60->3.70->4.0.

Another way, which may be the best way, is to contact your
Partner or Microsoft Support for the local region and get the best
available method to upgrade.

INDEX

.fib, 36
.NET, 29

Aging inventory, 76
allocation, 45, 87
archive capabilities, 70

Binary Large Object, 15
BLOB, 15, 37, 68
bmp file, 15

C/AL, 23, 29, 30, 48, 103
C/SIDE, 15, 29, 111
cfront, 34
change the color, 49
Check Stub, 100
Citrix, 46, 47
Closing sales orders, 83
Codeunit, 74, 111
CSV text, 18
currency, 7, 70, 80
customer #, 86
Customer Comments, 37
customer list, 71

dataport, 14, 18, 33, 73,
    75, 105, 107, 111
Dataport, 12, 14, 111
date, 16
delete customers, 81
Detail Trial Balance
    report, 24
Disaster Recovery, 67
DOC folder, 11

domain group, 110

editable property, 103
Error 1355, 84
Excel, 24, 50, 65, 73, 74,
    75, 107, 108, 109

Formatting, 77

Gregorian, 16

hidden files, 86
Hijri, 16
http, 106

Import data, 107
installation, 15, 25, 39,
    44, 59, 67, 113, 114
Inventory, 51, 88, 90, 94

journal entries, 82

license, 2, 30, 31, 32, 34,
    38, 50, 60, 63, 67, 83,
    85, 95, 96, 113, 114
logins, 21, 26, 110

Module 19, 84
MOM, 53
MS Access, 106

NAV 3.70, 86
NAV 4.0 SP2, 26, 28, 35
NAV 5.0, 25, 39, 44, 51
NAV4.0 SP3, 39

Navision 4., 92, 100, 106

Object Designer, 12, 36,
    46, 103
ODBC, 38, 53, 76, 106
OnLookup, 19
Outlook, 7, 39, 44, 48

passwords, 26
path string, 66
print, 24, 30, 45, 64, 72,
    74, 81, 94, 100, 102
print to excel, 24
printers, 64, 94
Purchase order, 70

RAID 1, 40
recurring journal, 45
remote desktop
    connection, 11
remote server, 11
reports, 7, 24, 47, 67, 70,
    78, 100
restoration, 67

sales invoice, 71, 95, 96,
    103
scroll bar, 42
SIC, 12

SP3, 22, 35, 39, 42, 56,
    57, 105, 116
SQL, 8, 13, 21, 25, 26, 31,
    40, 41, 42, 50, 53, 56,
    67, 82, 101, 105, 110,
    114
synchronization, 110

tab delimited, 105, 111
Terminal Server, 59
Transfer Order, 19

UEI, 107, 108
uninstall, 114
Universal Excel Importer,
    107

VAT, 75
Vista, 22, 25, 55, 56, 58

Windows Vista, 22, 55,
    56, 58
Windows XP, 21
WIP, 78

zup, 13, 14, 27, 47, 84, 86,
    94, 114
zup file, 13, 27, 47, 84,
    86, 114

www.ingramcontent.com/pod-product-compliance
Lightning Source LLC
Chambersburg PA
CBHW051057050326
40690CB00006B/751